BLESSINGS:

Pursuing a Spiritual Life

POEMS BY KATHERINE THERESE CECILIA EATMON

May - November 2012

Photography 2012 by Katherine T. Eatmon
Photograph for Grandma's Trooper curtesy of
Jim and Pat Vermeulen

ISBN: 978-1-300-39697-0
Raleigh, North Carolina
USA

Infinite Gratitude to those who
accompany me, love me and teach me:

My sisters—Mary, Monica, Pat, Patricia,
Rita, and Sabina
My brothers-Ethan, Jim, Kenny, Orion,
and Peter and my son-in-law—Jeremy

My family far and wide

My friends--Anne, Arlene, Bailey, Cindy,
Claire, Connie, Doreen, Eric, Esther, Gayle,
Jennifer C, Julie S, Kathy Jo, Kay H, Kay W,
Lori, McKenzie, Miki, Pam, Phil, Sharon,
Sheena, Shelagh, Susan P. and Tommy D.

The LEGACIES CARTEL: Andrea, Bonnie,
Caroline, Deb, Delphi, Felicia, Holly,
Jennifer H, Julie P, Lee, Nan, Rhonda,
Sherry, Tanya and Valerie

My guides—Michelle Poppe, and Douglas
Hammer

Sweet Junie

And all of you in THE rooms

Also by Katherine T. Eatmon

Peripheral Vision: Life on the Edge of Death (2009)

Right Here: Living an Ordinary Life (2011)

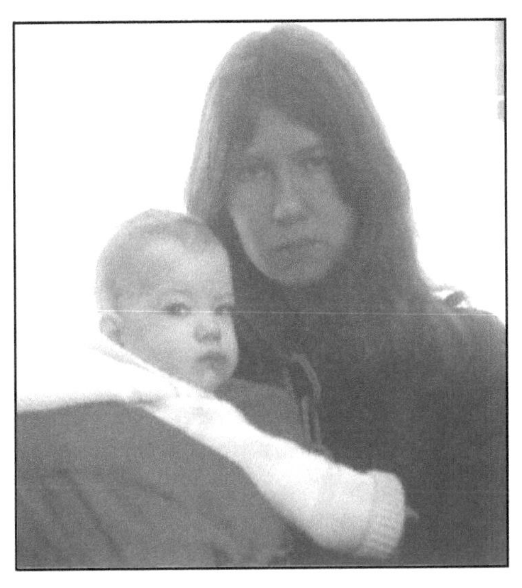

For my baby girl, Rachel Anna

and my baby boy, Oscar III

Blessed are they who mourn,
for they shall be comforted.
(Matthew 5:4)

Poems

Lourdes

Sleepless since three,
I first heard their invocation at five.
Lake birds chanting
Their clamorous appeal.
What birds are they who comfort me
With their litany?

I have lost God again,
Tumbling down into
The anguished grotto,
I gouge the plants and soil,
A visionary seeking His verdant spring.

There is no cure for this heartbreak,
Grief lingers like soil under my fingernails.

So I listen instead to this morning benediction
Trusting that they pray for me.

May 15, 2012

Orion

Emerging from my dense forest,
I regard a celestial sky
spanning the indigo horizon.
I collapse to the grass
Dizzied by its breadth.
Nearby lake creatures welcome me
with their discordant lullabies.
It is queerly comforting.

The Hunter stands guard over the murky lake.
Is it his vigilance
that keeps me on shore?
Is it his strength
that sustains me?

I have no hope to do the impossible,
Grasping for life like this
to the sharp shadowed emerald blades
beneath me.
Grief bleeds from my stigmata into the dewy earth.

At the brink of the insurmountable,
I reach to the stars and chant with the bullfrogs.
I cannot walk on water
like Orion and Jesus.
I can only hang on to this spinning orb
Under a sky filled with sparkling miracles
And listen
Waiting.

June 16, 2012

New Jeans (For Tom)
"God is subtle, but He is not malicious." Albert Einstein

You said you have a vision.
You see change as God's way of making space
For better things in your life.

I tried on that thought
Like size 6 designer jeans.
I stepped into it
Carefully, snugly
One foot at a time.

It clung to me tightly
And I felt my breath squeeze out as I zipped it up.

There. It's on.

It's hard to believe that this conforms.
It's agonizing!
How can this ache be a blessing?

Only time will tell...
For now I wear these strange jeans,
Pretending they fit.
I entertain God's promise
"This or something better...."

Perhaps.

June 16, 2012

Polliwogs

(For Oscar who would be 57 today)

The lake is murky here by the shore,
Saged with brush and bracken.
I recall children squatting nearby
And strain for a closer look.
My venerable hazel eyes take time to focus
But at last behold tiny transparent tadpoles
Squirming through the dingy mire.
Dozens of them!
City girl that I am, I am amazed at this
Haphazard congregation of polliwogs.

I sense a deep chuckle,
The laughter of my country boy husband
Watching me marvel in my jazzy sneakers.
His husky almond feet were not meant for shoes,
But for deep grass, black creeks and dusty roads.

He would not crouch at the edge like this.
Skin stained chestnut by the summer sun,
He would dive into the cool mystical algae,
Unafraid of the creatures scattering below him.

This thought makes me grin
As I stand at the edge of my new uncharted world,
A barefoot whippersnapper as my muse.

June 19, 2012

Still Dark

Four-thirty AM.
The beagles are eager to explore
Dragging me fiercely
As they snuffle and snort at the pavement.
They perceive a presence
Invisible to me.
How can they sense something
In this Cimmerian cavern?

I follow blindly
Sleepless once more
As always...
As I have been for seven weeks.

I don't know what today might bring
Afraid as I am of the unknown.
But the hounds thrust ahead bravely
Confident for me, and self assured.
I have no choice but to ensue.

June 23, 2012

Touch

"Daughter, your faith has healed you,
go in peace, and be freed from your suffering." Mark 5:34

Sister Dorothy Ann embraced me when my father died.
She swathed me in her yards of black habit
Whispering solace.
The ache in my heart was unbearable
But I did not weep.

When my husband was dying
I grasped his rough lifeless hand,
Whispered soothing prayers.
But I did not weep.

For decades I have grown worse,
Enduring lonely anguish.
I have dodged the tsunamic agony of contact,
Like a feral creature.

Ebbing as such, with my last hope,
I reached through the array
And touched you faintly, fearfully.
Your kind response was an antidote to my grief.

Now I bawl shamelessly, publically.
But you blanket me gently, protectively;
A loving presence throughout my day.

I am healing.

June 25, 2012

Moon shadow

They yank me toward the placid lake,
These ornery hounds.
Dewy grass dampens my feet
As I reluctantly pursue.
We move from the flagrant street lights
Into the nether light of newly night
And there is the shift.

Gibbous moon hovers over the hill,
Gifting me its shadow.
Even my brutes are stunned by its humble radiance
Pausing to sniff the nebulous impression.

The heavenly orb guides me through my phases.
It's been two months now
And I am waxing, too.
How did it happen, this amorphous change in me?
From stark anguish to dull ache.

My precious pets pull me forward
Untroubled by my vacillating moods.
They instinctively know
We are safe beneath the cycling sky.
For now I just abide.

June 28, 2012

Jesus Wept

(For my angels)

When I confessed my grief
I watched your weather change,
Bleak storm clouds rolling in
Just before the rain.
A flash behind your eyes;
Compassion and rage.
We touched.

You could not resurrect
What had expired weeks before
So instead you lingered,
Sharing my anguish.
Your empathy sheltered me.

Steadfast in our emerging rapport,
I dry my tears.
This despicable death will not drown me.

It takes time to turn from the dreary tomb,
And move toward dawn.
It is a different kind of awakening.
Prisms shimmering through the stalling deluge,
I remove my hands from the stone
And shift,
Dazed.

You remain.

July 2, 2012

<u>Caught</u>
(for my people)

For months you had been coming,
Amiable women folk,
Approaching me.
I dallied like a graceful chestnut deer
At a still grey lake,
Eyeing you cautiously.
Scared as I am,
I kept my safe distance,
At alert,
Ready to bound into the dense lush foliage.
Dire clouds threatened but instead I feared you.

The vicious tempest took me by surprise,
A violent onslaught that propelled me to the precipice.
I wailed into the bottomless void, lost.
I pleaded, begged, clawed the earth
Off balance and broken.

But there you were,
Arms open, catching me.
You had been waiting all along.

Soft whispers…
"We got you,
You're alright,
That's it, we're here.
We got you."

Soft whispers in the blinding darkness
Soothe me as I heal.
I am caught.
Saved.
Protected.

July 6, 2012

Thunder Moon

For Claire, Kathy Jo and Sheena

The night of the Thunder Moon
Was dismal, no light in sight.
But it is a moody month nonetheless.

Convening In the clammy car
Beneath the deluge,
Emotions swirl like a cyclone.
I regard their resounding ebb and flow,
As spates of rain assault our haven.
I cherish this difficult moment.

Your eyes reflect vacillating weather,
Shades of moss, topaz, and cobalt
Streaked with tears.
My sage eyes smile back.
I know this storm will end.
I know a new one will ensue
As mine do
As mine do.

I reassure you in the gloom,
Under a thunderous sky.
I comfort you in your desperate tempest.
We will endure this.

Together.

July 7, 2012

God's Hands

The teal pool is calm, welcoming.
I descend into the balmy water,
Surprised at its warmth.
No reason to fight this bliss
I slide swiftly into its rapturous embrace.

I float on the surface, deafly,
Trustingly.
The cerulean sky rotates silently overhead
Cirrus stripes charting my dreamy course.

Once again You refused to let me drown
Despite my insistence and despair.
You clutched me until there was no struggle left,
Till I realized
There was nothing to fear in this heavenly place.
At long last safe and quiet in Your ever-changing arms,
I'm light as the bees that visit me.

This moment lasts forever,
Your enduring smile constant
As the shifting, spiraling sphere.

Right now, I can't help but smile, too.

July 9, 2012

Rainbow over Durham Freeway

(In Greco-Roman mythology, the rainbow was considered to be a path made by a messenger between Earth and Heaven.)

After three bleak days
The sun breaks thru
The braided clouds.
I push ahead,
This early evening,
Dodging bumps and billows
On my arduous road.
I am weary.

Unexpected and barely visible
A rainbow emerges aloft.
How long has it been there
Hovering over my highway?
Am I dreaming?
No, it is still there, barely.

I drive under an overpass
Into a downpour
And just as suddenly,
The apparition is gone.

What a pity!

But the lane remains,
A shimmering prism in my heart,
The messenger beside me
Riding toward the guiding light.

July 14, 2012

Purple Hearts

Dainty lavendar ceramic hearts
Pierced my ear lobes 6 weeks ago.
Now they won't come out.
I pluck and pinch until my skin is flaming red
Still they don't budge.
Stuck.

I am stuck in a hateful place,
3 AM,
Memorizing the crape myrtle leaves.
Bitterness rustles like the wind
Outside my bedroom window.
Spite has stabbed my heart
Like stubborn studs.

After struggling head on for days,
I stop pulling.
I wriggle these tiny gold posts,
Bend and wiggle them
With my clumsy fingertips.
I coax them ineptly
Till at last they pop out.

So, too, with the relentless thorns
That have adhered to my heart.
This rage won't easily surrender.
But I prod and nudge
Hoping for progress,
Even if only for sleep next 3 AM.

July 14, 2012

Grazing Deer

We explode out of my apartment
Hounds dragging me relentlessly
Down the wooden steps.
Barking brutally
They pull and yank,
Toward some invisible foe.
Then I behold the comely tawny deer.
This moment is immensely immortal.

My boisterous beagles
Hurtle against their reins
Unsuccessfully.
The peaceful deer will have their grass.

Every day
I hurdle against a harrowing halter of my own,
A delusion I believed.
It fades in and out
As I wander through my restless days.

We skirt the neighborhood
Under the new moon
Toads and bullfrogs begging our presence.
Stars rotate overhead,
And still I want for those gangly dreamy creatures.

We round back and they remain,
Elegantly loitering.
Like my vague voyage,
There is no denying this shadowy reality.

Still, I walk forward.

July 18, 2012

Raging Rain and Rainbow

For Kathy Jo and Sheena

Distracted by my frosty frappe,
And intimate conversation
I didn't mind the growing gloom.
Thunder awakens me to a storm.
"OMG, we will be late!"
We dodge the downpour,
Launch our cars,
And hurtle to the meeting.

How can this be?
Raging rain raps my roof,
But there, up ahead,
Shimmering over the trees
Hovers a rainbow!
I swerve as I snap
But capture the phantom.
YES!

I drift toward the unexplored,
Grappling with opposing realities.
Grief and Relief.
Sorrow and solace.
Pain and pleasure.

Need I proof
That light and darkness
Exist side by side?

There.
I have it.

July 21, 2012

Waxing Moon

Low in the sky
Bright but slight
Suspends the waxing moon.

I spot it in Durham,
Emerging
From the haze over the road.
Remarkable!

I hasten home to Raleigh
Searching all the way.
Arrive,
Rush the dogs out to the lake.

No moon.
Just the smug stars.

I know it is there,
I have seen it.
Though now it hides,
I know it is there.

Thus is my life.
The answers will appear when I need them.

They are there, just out of reach.
Like tonight's shrouded moon.

July 22, 2012

Purgatory

(For those who find themselves in a condition of being open to God, but still imperfectly, the journey towards full beatitude requires a purification, which the faith of the Church illustrates in the doctrine of "Purgatory"- Catechism of the Catholic Church)

I am fully awake
Serenaded by the accolades
Of tufted titmice, blazing cardinals
And stained-glass blue jays
Before I notice.

It is quiet.

Thirteen weeks, lost in limbo,
Done.
That incessant rumination,
Purged.

I gaze dreamily
Through my sacred crape myrtle leaves
At the glorious day,
Grown holy
By the prayers of the faithful.

The birds witness my ascent.
Where to now?
The heaven of today.

July 29, 2012

Mourning Doves

Cirrus feathers
Cloak the waning western moon
Cumulus clouds
Conceal the eastern rising sun.
I behold the two stars
As I walk my eager beagles.
They dodge in and out of vapor
Like hounds pursuing a fresh scent.

I move between night and day,
Gloom and glow, fluently,
Navigating my wavering weather.
I skirt moody lakes and mournful songs
Stalking the unknown.
Pressing on despite turmoil
Is new to me.

I trail my willing dogs,
As the shining orbs
Break out.

We travel through radiance,
Regardless.

August 5, 2012

Letting Go

In my recurring dream
I drop the beryl leash.
My copper cloaked hound leaps out of reach
Then turns, staring daringly.
He refuses to return,
Of course.

I wake to loss daily,
The intimacy I assumed bridled
Drifting into illusion.
I cannot surrender
This conniving beast,
It roams feral thru my infinite days
And endless nights.

I ramble, also,
Searching for that stray pet,
A passion I never really did possess.

There will be no relieved reunion,
For what I chase did not exist.
There is, however
The promise of something better.

But I must let go the lead.

August 7, 2012

Broken Wing

The dappled thrasher
Warbles its awful song
As it wobbles across the timbers
Near my apartment.
I approach cautiously
But it skitters, screeching,
Just out of reach.
The angry storm must have
Flung it against the wet walls,
Fracturing its fragile wing.
I trail the flailing bird
But it stays distant
And scolding.

It is dank and late
And I am weary.
The tawny cripple
Flutters frantically down the staircase
To the floor below.

Turning away from this turmoil,
I accept that
I cannot mend those feathers,
For I tend my own severed bough.
I enter my front door
Gratefully.

Healing.

August 10, 2012

Lost Keys

While shepherding the slobbering hounds
My keys were swallowed
By the shimmering emerald blades spiking
The savvy hill.
Or so I thought.

Crisscrossing and scouring the verdant sward
Rendered no results.
I fought despair.

I struggle with despair daily
Searching my shallow pockets for
My lost romance.
Wandering fretfully
Through fierce terrain,
It's clear
I pursue an illusion.

I abandon my grassy quest,
Resting in quiet.
Then I remember,
The keys are in a closet pocket.

Yep! There they are.

I realize all at once,
There has been no abandonment.
The intimacy I seek is
Right here.
Inside me.
Nothing went awry.

Just like my keys.

August 18, 2012

Perennials
(I fell apart, but got back up again.—30 seconds to Mars)

No matter the weather,
Stinging heat
Or pounding downpour,
These blissful petunias boundlessly bloom.
Today their pinks and purples
Droop under the downpour.

I open the patio door
To entertain the refrain of fresh rain.
Daisy drifts in and out for a look.
Like the lively blossoms
She pays no mind to the dank deluge
That drenches her copper and black coat.

We sit like this
Flowers, hounds and I
Immersed in our own musings.
The wet dog huddles
Under a towel beside me
Nurtured and warm.
Feelings wash over me,
Rushing rivulets down a hill.

No matter my weather
I withstand assaults,
Drying off and rising up
Again and again.
Is there an alternative to enduring?

The petunias think not.

August 19, 2012

I Feel Nothing

(To no one in particular)

After five years of devotion
I feel nothing for you.
You ripped my guts out
Ground them into dust,
And I feel nothing for you.

Why should I?

Those tender feelings are far flung memories,
Tugging at my vulnerable heart strings.
But I look at you
And I feel
Nothing.
Nothing for you.

Seeing you yesterday
Trudging with stooped shoulders
Out the room,
Not looking back,
I felt nothing.

You are nothing to me,
A faded photograph,
A lost ticket stub,
Something that slipped my mind.

All those endless nights
Whispering in the shadowy dark....
Are
Nothing to me.

Do you hear me?
You are nothing to me now.
Nothing.

August 19, 2012

Meteorology
(for Oscar III)

This week's hazy mournings
Reflect my dreary mood.
Somber nights smudge the waxing moon.
I meander through these dismal days
Feigning acquiescence.
My best is good enough.

My towering offspring
Scrutinizes my discontent.
His surly self hovers silently,
Spreading his supple arms
To pat my aging back.
We have traversed eons and oceans
To reach this humble place.

As the warm front passes
I heed a ding,
Catch the flash that
Traveled outer space
Bounced off circling satellites
Cut through stratus clouds
And landed in my worn hand.
My bristly boy's text
Years in coming,
Pierces my mist:
"I Love You."

With that my wind shifts,
My fog clears.
My best is good enough.

August 24, 2012

Moonlight on Lake

Blue moon, they say,
Two moons in one month.
I skirt the lake at dusk
Glorifying the glow rising
Above the grove.

I revel in twilight radiance,
Delight in a moon shadowed lawn.
It is my second chance
To find pleasure in ambiguity,
Cleaving the past
And the future
All at once.

The dual moon is blue and blush.

As am I.

September 1, 2012

Self Love
(inspired by Julie)

I might be addicted to this,
Half naked, smiling, and supine
Beside the manganese blue pool.
Solar heat sears my skin
Beneath a mirrored sky.
I feel like a teenager,
Tan for the first time in
Almost 6 decades.

Feigning sleep,
I regard the gentle lap of chlorine water,
Feel fiery breath on my skin.
A sweet dream teases my sensual trance.

Suddenly, a light caress on my breast...

What?
I am still alone.
No lover hovers.

But there on my buff bosom is the clue,
A frail rosy blossom
Shaken from the nearby crape myrtle.

Yes, I might be hooked on this,
Lying luxuriously beneath a lovely shedding tree.

Healing.

September 2, 2012

Autumn Light
(For Adam Michael)

Born in the north east
You navigated the seasons
Down south.
Pudgy progeny,
Sensitive from the womb,
You took your steps tentatively
Scolding every stumble.

We have walked together
For nineteen splendid autumn lights.
Now you tower over me,
Sparse beard fringing your chin.
I cannot catch you anymore
When you plunge into your abyss,
But this time you seize my hand,
Pleading with your piercing blue eyes,
And hold on.

I got you, baby.

September 8, 2012

Charlotte
(for Little Tommy Duane)

I strain to embrace you,
Balancing on tip toe to savor the feel
Of your soft cheek again.
We embrace like this tightly,
Forty years later,
Despite the weight
And aches we have gained.
I follow your gentle hands,
Gesturing expressively as you speak.
Amazing that we share the same language.

Still.

Still you know me.
How is that so after all these years?
Your words make me laugh and weep,
Your eyes see my heart.

Still.

What could we have become
Had we shared everything?

We kiss goodbye,
Your swift lips soft and moist.

No matter,
What we have become
Right now, here,
Is remarkable.

September 8, 2012

Night Chorus
(would have been my 12th wedding anniversary)

There is a playground close by
With slide and swings.
I walk the eager hounds
Then loop back
To recline onto the sticky slide.
The night creatures sing.
I wonder,
"Would anyone care if I die here
Under this dense tree?"
My beagles strain against their leads
But I am rooted.
Who would care
If this were my last night?
It's so dark...
Sometimes headlights pass, yet
Crickets soothe me.
In this twilight sleep
The late summer wind whispers,
Finally
And clearly
"I do."

I rouse and allow the pesky dogs
To yank me home.
I have my answer.
It's right here.

September 15, 2012

Shooting Star

Tornado clouds ashen the sapphire sky
On the miles home from Durham.
Night arrives before me
Blessed by fleecy feathers streaking overhead.
I pause in the newly autumn evening
to watch their swift passing.
Alit,
I feel drunk as the dome
Swirls over me.
And there it is,
A spark,
A shimmer
Of a star
Shooting through the clouds.
Could it be?
I am unsure
As the firmament
Surges above.

I would like to believe
I witnessed a fireball
As testament of...

Something...

I will just have to wonder
Walking through these shrinking days
And swelling nights.

September 20, 2012

Wildflowers
(All is well, and all shall be well
and all manner of things shall be well.
Julian of Norwich)

Tiny canary blooms
Pop up seemingly suddenly
Beneath my feet.
The grass carpet saturates my sneakers
As I squat to admire my surprise,
Quints of sunshine
I'd almost missed
After a restless night.

This elusive marvel,
Graces my walk today
Like a morning star
At dawn.

No matter my wet shoes,
It is worth the reminder

That all I need
Is right here.

And it is divine.

September 25, 2012

Blue Heron

(For Rachel)

Still dark
The silhouette is clear,
Compelling.
A blue heron dozing in the shallow lake
Attracts my attention.
I am paralyzed despite the pull
Of my curious hounds.
For not even half a minute
We exist together,
But dismayed by my unruly mutts
The charming creature
Spreads its spacious wings,
Leisurely skims the dim lake
And glides into the mist.

It is like this with my beloved daughter,
Sudden sightings, fleeting contacts
Graced by her contagious, lyrical laughter,
Then drifting back to her world.

I treasure these brief seconds of intimacy,
Locking eyes and hearts with those I love
Then letting them fly.

October 3, 2012

The Kiss

For Oscar Jr.

It was one of those real dreams.
You and I were barely touching but
So close I felt your breath on my face.
Hypnotized, our lips touched,
Pressed, explored.
You were gentle, caring.
I reached up to put my peach arms
Around your wide almond neck,
(So familiar!)
And you pulled me against your expansive chest
As we kissed passionately, lovingly.

When I woke we were still kissing.
I roused, disoriented,
Surprised at your absence.
Where did you go?
Off on one of your nightly desertions?

This is no momentary leaving,
You have been gone seven years,
Resting under the silk daffodils
I place at your grassy grave.

This mourning is as if you never left.
Your lips linger for hours,
Your memory lives in my heart
Forever.

October 3, 2012

The Other Side of the Lake

It is as if the lake overflows its shores
The grass is so wet.
We skirt it briskly,
Beagles battling their leads
As I endure our walk.
A crowd of dappled geese and hooded mallards
Glide back and forth as we edge closer.
We trouble them
Though we bear no threat.
I have firm hold on these leashes.
I cannot blame them.
I am troubled, too,
By my ailing daughter.
The threat of loss edges closer
As I elude it.
Again.
Yet again.

I loop the pond.
The creatures outlines are blurry
Against the glassy morning surface.

I come full circle
As a streak of light startles me.
There behind me emerges the sun
On time as usual
More brilliant than ever.

It accompanies me and the fowl
As we dodge our fears and worries.
Day by day.
Moment by moment.

October 15, 2012

Grandma's Trooper
For Rachel

At four years old
My adorable baby girl developed cancer.
Malignancy broiling in her preschool brain.
She twirled like a ballerina
Through the regiment,
Mom and I applauding her feat
With curtain calls and ovations.
Her performance was flawless.

Twenty three years later
The lethal cells are back.
My aging hand on my baby's shoulder,
We face the grave surgeon's news.

Moments of despair last forever,
Then I see the transformation...
Shadows fall from her face
As she arrays herself in her emotional finery
Rising visibly on the exam table.
I feel Mom's perfect presence fill the room
Approvingly.
And my darling woman makes her declaration:
There will be no gloom here.

She says she prefers to dance!

October 16, 2012

<u>Autumn Morning</u>

It's not yet dawn
When I walk the dogs.
The entire universe hovers and
I am dizzy with star gazing.
Mercury, Jupiter and Orion
Flank me as I stagger.
They will not let me falter.

There is nothing I can do now
But wait.
Toddle this tightrope and wait.

The Gods grace me with their care
Reminding me
Endlessly that
All shall be well.

No matter what.

October 27, 2012

Bird Songs and Church Bells

The distant typhoon
Worries the crape myrtle boughs
Outside my open bedroom window.
They fret and fuss
Waking me hourly with their anxious whispers.
I am restless, too,
Troubled by my impending tempest.

The last time I rouse
I have company;
A fiery cardinal balances on the branches,
Chanting kindly.
And for the first time in this comfy berth
I hear church bells
Pealing blindly.
I drift gently, caressed by dawn's winds.

I linger in this safe place
Listening to the swelling morning.
The air is chill
But I am ready.

Prepared.

October 28, 2012

Mom's Rosary
(For Sabina, who found them)

I forgot how to pray,
It's been so long since I went to Mass.
So I google: "how to pray the rosary"
On my Ipad.
Everyone has gone to lunch
But I sit here
Stubbornly,
In the stately surgical waiting room.
The beige beads are warm in my fingers
As I count off.
Hail Mary, full of Grace....

I don't feel her blessings now
Images of fire
And flood flashing on the flat screen.
I feel hurricane winds and downpours
Of despair inside me.

So I count off again,
Imploring,
Reciting the now familiar words,
Blessed are you amongst women...

The precious fruit of my womb
Is in the hands of skilled surgeons.
I appeal over and over
Ten, twenty, thirty,
Sixty, one hundred,
One hundred and twenty times.

Now and at the hour of our death
Amen.

November 4, 2012

<u>God Smiled</u>
(Inspired by Dr. Hammer)

Just out of surgery
Profound pain is palpable
On her pitiful face.
She whimpers. "It hurts!"
Tears flowing from her precious eyes.
But she lives.

She will survive.

This is the third time
I almost lost her.
At birth, at four
And now at twenty seven…
I caress her soft pricked hand
And whisper solace.
Yes, I weep too.

It's hard to believe
That such a moment
Could be so splendid,
Nurses hovering,
Machines beeping,
Lives balancing on the edge…
But it is.

Over and over,
I have witnessed the beauty
Of this lovely child's life
Prevailing.

And I know
Without a doubt
God is smiling, too.

Again.

www.ingramcontent.com/pod-product-compliance
Ingram Content Group UK Ltd.
Pitfield, Milton Keynes, MK11 3LW, UK
UKHW041832200726
13854UKWH00003BA/1109